Life's

Nita Jayne

BookLeaf
Publishing

Presentation by *BookLeaf Publishing*

Web: www.bookleafpub.com

E-mail: info@bookleafpub.com

ISBN: 9789395755931

First edition 2022

DEDICATION

I would like to dedicate this book to my family:

My son Thomas & partner Jennie

My son Daniel & wife Heather & my Grandson Freddie

My son Michael & wife Jade & my Grandson George

I love you all much xxx

ACKNOWLEDGEMENT

I'd like to thank all who I've met on life's
journey.
Special thank you's to Malcolm Yates and Alice
Seagrave for support and
encouragement.

Thank you to Alice Seagrave for the illustration
"Spud" and to Michael Jephcott for the
illustration "Sprout" for the poem
Spud & Sprout and the Morris Men.
Thank you to all my family and to Barbara for
being my sister.
I love you all so much.

PREFACE

I have written poems all my life. This book is a
collection of poems written from the age of 13 to
the present day.
Some are personal, emotional. Some are silly.
Some have been written for others as requested.
Just something I wanted to do.

I Love You

Tomorrow we may not be together
We may fade with the evening sun
Only time will tell
Cherish each moment we share
For they are tokens of love
Eternal as a memory
We cannot know the future
So each day we are together
Each moment far or near
Always remember
I love you

Flowers

I was like a flower in winter
When you came it was spring
You smiled and my petals opened
You freed me and my heart could sing
You're my sun, my rain. You are my life
 I reach out to the love you bring
And unlike flowers that wither and die
Our love remains eternally spring

Waiting

I waited so long ...

For a smile that warms me
Like soft rays from the sun
A smile, lovingly lingering
When I'm alone

For a touch that frees me
From my mind
A touch, teasingly tingling
Tender and kind

For a kiss that excites me
And trembles with dare
A kiss, slowly caressing
Gentle with care

For words that thrill me
No matter how few
Words, softly whispering
Lasting and true

For a person to share
Through laughter and tears
A person, lifting my joy
Weakening my fears

For someone to hold me
And never let go
Someone, there always
Loving me so

I waited so long...

And then there was you

Count on Me

If you count all the stars
In a clear night sky
That's how many days
I will need you

If you count the wild blossoms
In a summer meadow
That's how many ways
I want to please you

If you count all the raindrops
And a million more
That's how many times
I want to kiss you

If you count the grains of sand
Glistening on the shore
That's just how much that
I would miss you

If you count all the snowflakes
Of a winter's fall
That's how often I'd be there
If ever you should call

And you can count on me
For always and forever
For that's how long, my darling
I will love you

If Just This Night

If just this night you take my hand
And lead me to the stars
Forever it will stay with me
To cherish what was ours
Not knowing what tomorrow brings
Or where our lives will go
I'll hear your whispered words of love
As gentle breezes blow
I'll give to you myself this night
My passion, love and heart
Knowing that the dawn will come
And we will have to part

Looking for Love

Where are you?
Why can't I find
Someone just for me
One of a kind
I'm searching for you
I'm so lonely each day
You must be out there
Feeling the same way

Where are you?
Just let us meet
Take my unfinished life
And make it complete
For should I die
Without knowing love
Then heaven must wait
I could not go above

Where are you?
My soul's in despair
I'm living without you
When you should be here
Is it not promised
Is it not fate
One day I'll find you
My true soul mate

Trust Untrust

My heart has been alone for so long
Just going with the flow
Not bothered how it goes
But not knowing where to belong

It's easy, it's for the best, it won't get broken
And if anyone tried to care
My heart gets scared
Of any heartfelt words that could be spoken

Promises turn to lies, dreams don't come true
It's better to be alone
When all is said and done
So I understand if you feel the same way too

We've both been hurt before, demons from the
past
And it still hurts
Invisible scars, deep cuts
We can't trust the future, we know it wouldn't
last

And it's so sad because I think I could love you
You'd be my world
'til we grew old ...
You see, there's still some mindless hope in my
solitude

Kack & Me

We were aged four. Playing in the street
I was dragging Percy in a box
You said "Will you be my friend?"
I said " I'd rather not !"
Well we've been firm friends ever since
Do you remember back in the day
You, me, Lizeth and the boys
Mischief, footie and play
Old Sherlock chasing us up the road
As we climbed his trees and looked for toads
Down the track and blackberry picking
Selling flowers that we'd been nicking
Icecream Joe. Cor! Starsky and Hutch
The bullies in the bush, you beat 'em up!
Tea on a Sunday. Sweet nanny plaster
Hide the rag in the laundrette - time would go
faster
Lizzie and Benji walking up for the pink
We fetched the horse muck so Dad's roses would
stink
That day in the park. We had a nice picnic
Well it was 'til you frisbee'd my biscuits
At school we had to write what we'd cooked
But I couldn't as you was cooking my book

And in the library whilst trying to study
You're a German spy - my one crazy buddy
The bestest days, I'll never forget
I'm my life you're the best person I've met
Of your friendship I'll never have enough
My soul friend, you - my Mason scruff

For Rachael Holly & Amy

Amy

Whenever a butterfly appears 🦋
I wonder if you are somewhere near
Showing your colours. Fluttering your wings
Dancing around the birds as they sing
Your sweet personality shining through
Doing all the things you couldn't do
Chasing rainbows, twinkling the stars
Dancing around the beautiful flowers
Fluffing up clouds, rustling trees
Sweet raindrop kisses, sending love in the
breeze
So dearest child when a butterfly appears
I wonder if you're somewhere near 🦋

Robbie

My friend next door is Robbie
He's Scottish, och aye the noo!
If he wasn't living next door
I don't know what I'd do
He lends a hand with anything
He loves me as a mother
I shout " Robbie get your arse round here"
And he shouts "Aye, nae bother"
We chat and laugh through many days
Although he's often feeling low
He gives himself a hard time
But he's one of the nicest guys I know
And if you want to find him
He'll be lying on the 'green'
A spliff hanging from his fingers
Shouting " Awa an bile yer heid."

FOR MY SONS Tom Daniel and Michael xxx

My newborn cradled in my arms
So innocent and small
You are perfect in every way
I'm overwhelmed with so much love

My toddler sitting on my knee
Your infectious cheeky smile
Chubby little hands clap with glee
If only you'd stay like this for a while

My little boy grown some more
Where will you go today
Lost in your imaginary world
I'm blessed to watch you play

My brave lad, first day at school
Running off without a care
I wave goodbye and turn to leave
Brushing away a wistful tear

My spotty kid at high school now
Tie undone, shirt hanging out
Being cheeky, testing the rules
Thinks he knows what it's all about

Now look at you a teenage dream
Checking the mirror- your biggest fan
Winking at girls making them scream
A cool boy racer in his 'tin can'

Suited and booted my smart young man
Off to work you go
Grown up, so independent
My pride just overflows

New house, new love. More proud tears
As you begin a whole new chapter
And wishing that you'll always have
A happy ever after

Looking back to the day you was born
I'm amazed at the man you've become
You've made your place in this uncertain world
And I'll love you forever....Your Mum xxx

Summer Garden

Just chilling in the garden
A pleasant glass of wine
Soaking up the sun's rays
Relaxed forgetting time
Sweet perfume from the meadow
Butterflies fluttering by
Bees busy collecting nectar
The breeze whispers a restful sigh
Birds sing their pleasant melodies
So heavenly to me
And my dog lazies sleepily
Beneath the blossom tree

For my Swimblers Rachael Courtney Debs and Sal xxxx

THE SAXON TREE

The tree stretched out its arms
As if to draw you in for a hug
Lean up against it, feel its strength
And smile at bird or rodent or bug
This tree has seen so many things
For hundreds of years or more
Children playing, swimmers swimbling
Lover's loving ...... war
Stood next to rumbling water
Of black and gold and green
Beneath swaying swirls and twirling leaves
And sun gleaming in between
Over lichened walls and stoney caves
Remembering life before
Crumbling down to the water's edge
To the river we adore
So cooling and so calming
Oh feeling total bliss
All who bathe beneath this beauty
Will embrace nature's soothing kiss

Christmas

ICY & SNOWY
  FIRE ALL GLOWY
WARM & COSY
  WOOLLY SOCK TOESIES
CHOCOLATEY TOESTIE
  CHESTNUTTY ROASTY
FAIRYLIGHT TWINKLES
  SUGAR SWEET SPRINKLES
GINGERBREAD SMELLS
  SOUND OF SLEIGHBELLS
CUDDLY & SNOOZY
  BERRIES & BOOZY
MISTLETOE KISSES
  CHRISTMASSY WISHES

For my Grandson's Freddie and George xx

SPUD & SPROUT & THE MORRIS DANCERS

Spud looked out of the window
Oh what a glorious day
"Come on Sprout, yer lazy mutt
Let's be on our way"

He started up the Dutchess
An old and curious barge
He smiled as he flung on his captain's hat
As he knew old Dutch was really in charge!

They drifted along the river ways
Waving to ducks as they paddled on by
They inhaled the perfumed breezes
And Dutch breathed a blissful sigh

Mumble Grumble upon Tumble
A funny name for a town
Sprout leapt off with the towrope
And moored Old Dutchess down

"We'll get some lunch" said Spud
Sprout woofed in delight
Food was just his favourite thing
He'd eat whatever was in sight

As they walked they heard strange music
It was such a peculiar noise
Jingle Jangle Clickety Clack
Jingle Jangle HOY!

It was the dancing Morris Men
Yay! Hurrah! Hee Hee!
Spud loved a bit of a jig
And he hopped about with glee

Bells on their shoes, swooshing bright scarves
And sticks clicking and clacking
All the folks in town gathered round
Some were skipping, some were clapping

Sticks ...Sticks...STICKS! Oh no
Sprout's most favourite thing
He leapt up grabbing a stick mid-clack
And ran off to bury his bling

In his haste he knocked over the music box
And everything flew up in the air
Smashing and crashing onto the floor
And scattering everywhere

Well the town folk were not happy
As all the music had stopped
But Sprout ran back with a key in his mouth
He found where his stick had dropped

"My My" said Mayor Mumble "he's found the key
To the music chest in the town hall
Come on everyone let's go there
We'll play music, one and all!"

Spud reached out for the fiddle
Fiddly diddly dee
A trombone, triangle, drums, horns and a whistle
Oompah ting ting bash thump honk wheeeeeee!

The whole town was dancing and singing
There was hot chocolate and jam donuts too
My favourite thing thought Sprout to himself
As they party'd the whole night through

Spud and Sprout went home to the Dutchess
Spud by the fire warming his toes
Sprout snuggled up on his cosy bed
Too tired to lick jam off his nose

For Ruben xx

I NEARLY FELL OFF MY UNICORN

Oh what pure beauty do I see
Of mountains strong surrounding me
Where rivers flow - mind go free
Sail on a ripple of fantasy
Trickle down past devil's gate
Where horrid creatures lie in wait
Warty noses, creepy gait
Dare to go? Accept your fate
And if you get to slug munchers style
Which could take you quite a while
But if you do be sure to smile
At toothless cringing crocodile
If you don't then you'll get stuck
In foul and filthy yucky muck
Where gummy Croc can try his luck
To get you and your bones he'll suck
Run, run fast to bottomless creak
Where pixies play at hide n seek
Close your eyes, you mustn't peek
If you see them you'll start to squeak
Like river rats that live below
A swishingly long tail will grow

And whiskers on your nose will glow
Sniffling snuffling to and fro
So blindly go to beasties lair
You could find a hairy bear
With snarling teeth and eyes that scare
Can you sneak on by beneath his glare
Until you reach the meadow haze
With faeries dancing among the maize
You can join them for a phase
Mystical carefree lazy days
Then dwindle down to rainbow dell
Unicorns drink from the coloured well
Shhh! It's a secret, you mustn't tell
Or you'll fall from Heaven and go to hell

House of Cards

The walls I build are fragile
Just like a house of cards
The slightest blow, the lightest knock
And I'm falling down so hard
My hopes and expectations
Of life. Of better things
Can be crushed as easily
As delicate butterfly wings
It's so hard to find the strength
To climb each wobbly stair
My efforts often crumble
My soul howling in despair
The further I fall the more I cling
To this threadbare spiralling rope
Because I know inside of me
Is Faith and Love and Hope

A Fibro of my Imagination

This illness is invisible, nobody can see
A possessing evil that lives inside of me
I'm laden with heavy chains as I go about my
chores
Weighed down with fatigue and foggy brain, my
body is so sore
So I try to take it easy, pace myself and rest
Then it's feels like burning, it's like it's a test
trying hard to break me, how much can I endure
And yes I am broken, at times can't take no more
The agony I live with I try not to let it show
I laugh and smile and play my part and you
would never know
So how can you believe me when I try to explain
That although I appear healthy, I'm always in
pain
It's invaded my whole body, it's taken control
From my head to my toes. My heart and yes my
soul
The person that I was before so happy and
carefree
Is trapped, bound and struggling - struggling to
be me
It's not just my body that this disease affects
Life with my loved ones it also tries to wreck

How can they understand what they can't see or feel
"Its in your head. Get over it. You're just lazy. It's not real
So I isolate, stay away. I feel so alone
I don't want to be a burden. I don't want to moan
I'm not looking for attention. I don't want sympathy
I'd just like understanding and you know that 'this' is me
I've had to come to terms with this, not easy to accept
So I'll move on to my next chapter and live with no regret

Be Kind

Others can't see inside my head
They don't know that I'm scared
My smile is saying I'm ok
 - as if anybody cared
...........they don't, do they?

Eyes can't lie, can they?
Aren't they windows to your soul
They say "are you ok?" as a tear sneaked out
" Oh it's nothing, just a cold"
..........but it is something

Hunched shoulders while sitting at my desk
I forgot body language is a giveaway
I sit up straight before I'm seen
Or say " I've got a bad back today"
...............always an excuse

"Hey, are you coming out tonight?
It's going to be such fun."
I would have liked to have gone
But I'm sat here all alone
.... I'm always alone in my tortured head

Who would want to be with me
When I am such a mess
On the outside I seem 'normal'
If only they could see my distress
.................I can't tell anyone

I don't want to be me
I want to be just like you
You can't break my barriers
They keep 'safe' what I'm going through
................I wish you could

All I'm saying is be aware
And if not, always be kind
Because you don't know who's tormented
By a fraught and f****d up mind
...............it might be you

BITTERSWEET CHRISTMAS from a Mother to her Son

I'll be missing you this Christmas
It just won't be the same
No setting at the table
No present with your name

Oh I'll get through it somehow
Love and laughter hide the pain
If I could only have one Christmas wish
You'd be here with me again

And I will never forget you
All the memories I hold dear
Precious moments spent together
Lots of love throughout the years

So I raise a glass to you my son
And I'll send you bittersweet cheers
I'll rock you always in my heart
And silently cry my tears

FROM A SON TO HIS FATHER

Is it too late to tell you
How much you meant to me
You were my rock. My idol
You were all that you could be
A Husband, Father, Grandad, Friend
The best you ever had
But to me, quite simply
You was just my Dad
Strong, steadfast, respected
True markings of a man
Yet kind and quietly spoken
I'll be like you Dad if I can
Head of our loving family
Now there's a chink in the chain
But I hope someday in another world
We could link up again
So we must go on without you
I can't believe you're gone
But Father you will live on
Inside the heart of your son

Ingram Content Group UK Ltd.
Milton Keynes UK
UKHW020920030423
419517UK00011B/1322